Germs Are Not for Sharing

Elizabeth Verdick

Illustrated by Marieka Heinlen

free spirit

PUBLISHING®

Library of Congress Cataloging-in-Publication Data
Verdick, Elizabeth.
    Germs are not for sharing / [text by Elizabeth Verdick ; illustrations by Marieka Heinlen].
        p. cm.— (Best behavior series)
    ISBN-13: 978-1-57542-197-1
    ISBN-10: 1-57542-197-6
  1. Hygiene—Juvenile literature. 2. Bacteria—Juvenile literature. I. Heinlen, Marieka. II. Title. III. Series.
    RA780.V47 2005
    613—dc22
                                                                          2005026220

Reading Level Grades 1–2; Interest Level Ages 4–7;
Fountas & Pinnell Guided Reading Level H

Cover and interior design by Marieka Heinlen

10 9 8 7 6
Printed in Hong Kong
P17200610

Free Spirit Publishing Inc.
217 Fifth Avenue North, Suite 200
Minneapolis, MN 55401-1299
(612) 338-2068
help4kids@freespirit.com
www.freespirit.com

Dedication

To the folks at Children's Hospital in St. Paul,
who took great care of my son Zach during two hospitalizations;
and to Zach himself, who is learning how to handle his asthma,
wash his hands while singing the alphabet,
and spread the word that germs are not for sharing.
—E.V.

For Mason, a great big brother who *never* coughs on his new baby sister,
and for Avery and Veronica, who are too tiny and squeaky clean
to know about germs yet.
—M.H.

Acknowledgments

We especially want to thank the following people for their expertise:

Gail Hansen, R.N., L.S.N., F.N.P., Minneapolis Public Schools

Bethany Malley, teacher, Sunshine Montessori Preschool, Minneapolis

Andrew Ozolins, M.D., Children's Hospitals and Clinics of Minnesota

Christine Pearson, Division of Media Relations,
Centers for Disease Control and Prevention

What are too small to see . . .
but can have the power to make you sick?

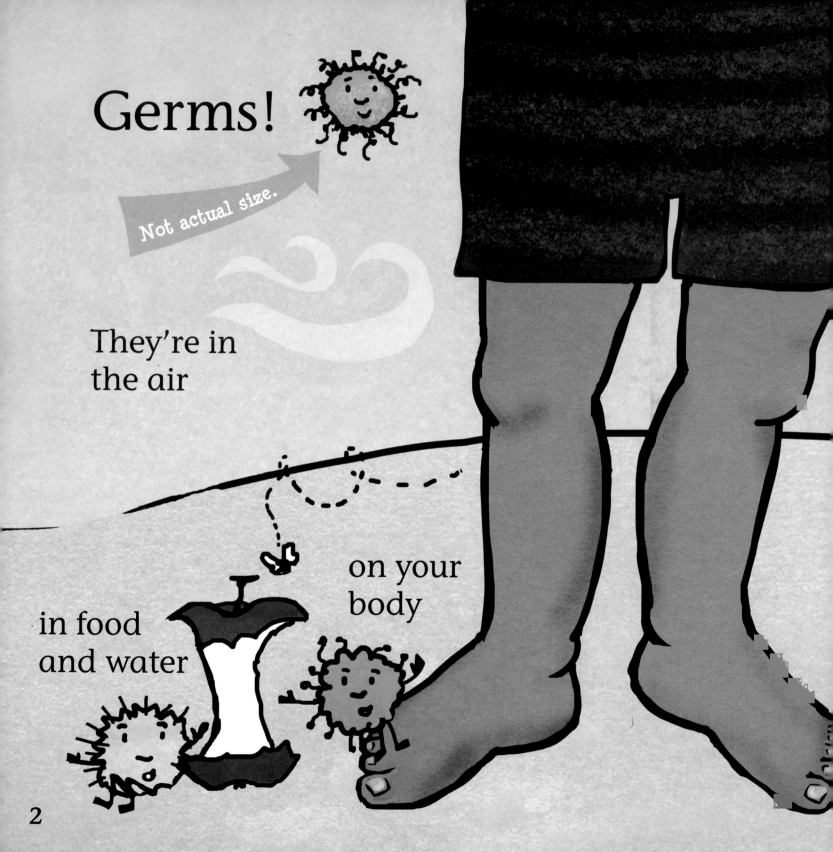

Still, germs are not for sharing

4

because germs can make you sick.

Achoo! Achoo! What do you need to do?
Cover your nose with a tissue
before the germs get out.

Blow, wipe, and toss.

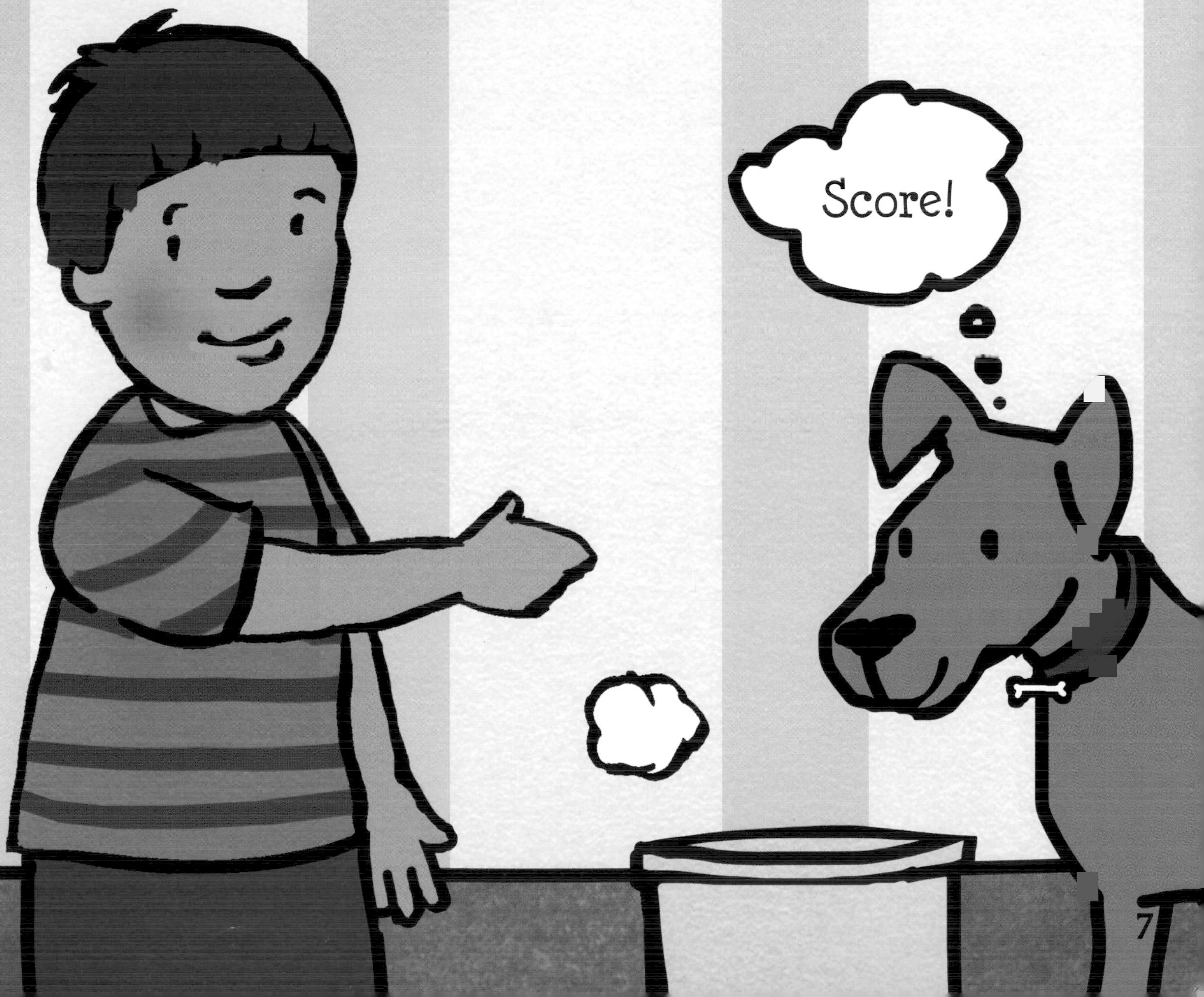

Cough, cough, cough!
What do you need to do?

Cover up
your mouth
before the
germs get out.

Like this

or this

or even like this.

9

If you cough or sneeze into your hands, hurry up and wash them because

Germs are not for sharing.

When germs get on your hands,
they can spread to other people.

When you hold hands

or play games

or give each other high fives.

Whenever you touch something,

your germs get left behind—and you might even pick up some new ones.

Here are some places where germs hang out:

17

Germs, germs everywhere . . .
what can you do?

You can wash your hands.

Use warm water and lots of soap,
scrub, scrub, scrub.

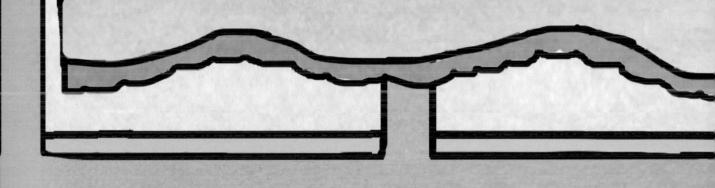

Wash for as long as it takes to sing the ABCs or Happy Birthday (twice).

Scrub the tops, scrub your palms,

wash under your nails,
and even your wrists.

Now
rinse,
rinse,
rinse...

Send those germs down the drain.

10 good times to wash your hands:

1. before you eat

2. after you eat

3. after you sneeze, cough, or blow your nose

4. after rubbing your eyes

5. after picking your nose

Yuck!

6. after playing outside or with pets

7. after counting your coins

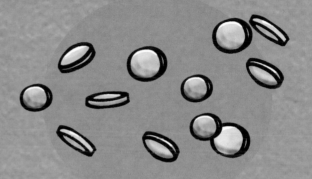

8. after crying

9. after using the bathroom

10. whenever they're dirty!

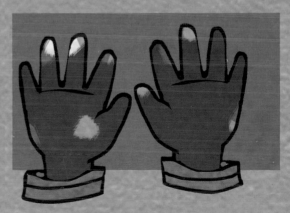

That's 10 good times to wash your hands—one for each finger.

ALL CLEAN!

A Few More Words About Germs

Grown-ups and kids can read this together!

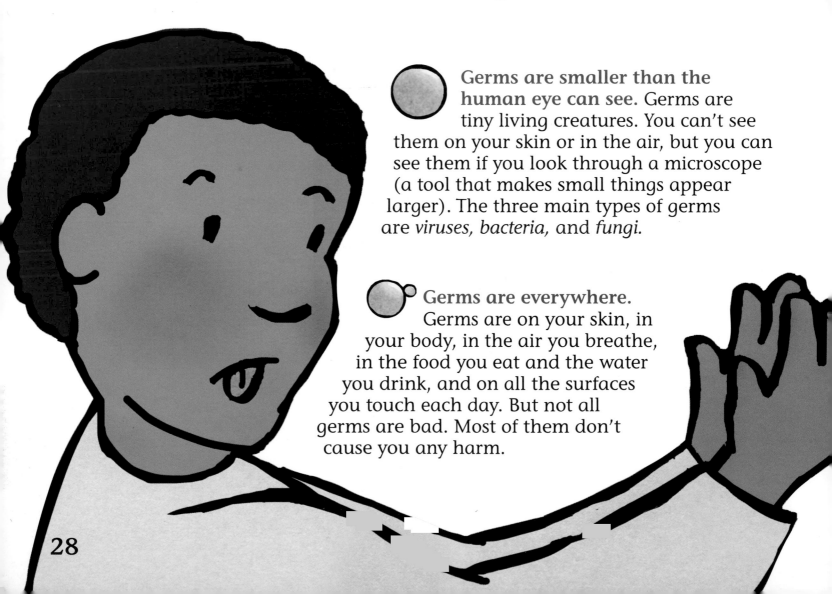

Germs are smaller than the human eye can see. Germs are tiny living creatures. You can't see them on your skin or in the air, but you can see them if you look through a microscope (a tool that makes small things appear larger). The three main types of germs are *viruses, bacteria,* and *fungi.*

Germs are everywhere. Germs are on your skin, in your body, in the air you breathe, in the food you eat and the water you drink, and on all the surfaces you touch each day. But not all germs are bad. Most of them don't cause you any harm.

Some germs can make you sick. You've probably had a cold, the flu, or an infection in your ear or throat. (In fact, kids catch more colds than anyone else.) It's no fun being sick! But your body has ways of fighting off illnesses so you can feel better. Sometimes, you may have to see a health care professional to get medicine to kill off the germs.

Your body is a germ fighter. Maybe you didn't know that your body has built-in defenses against harmful germs. Your eyelashes help trap germs before they get into your eyes. The hairs in your nose catch some of the germs you breathe in. Whenever you swallow, germs travel down to your tummy where the stomach juices can kill them. Your *immune system* is your body's disease-fighting system. It helps protect you from illness or allows you to get better when you're sick.

Germs can get in through your eyes, nose, and mouth. Some harmful germs *do* get in and make you sick. For example, if you have germs on your hands and then you rub your eyes, you're letting germs in. You can get germs if you suck your thumb or bite your fingernails, or if you pick your nose. And of course you can get germs if someone spits on you or if you kiss someone who's sick. There are lots of ways that germs get passed on from one person to the next. Just remember a few basics: *Noses are not for picking. Mouths are not for spitting. Thumbs are not for sucking. Fingernails are not for biting.* And one more thing: Brushing your teeth is a great way to keep your mouth cleaner!

Germs can get in through cuts and scrapes. You've probably fallen down and scraped your knees or elbows lots of times.

And maybe a grown-up showed you how to wash off the cut, which also washes away the germs. Anytime you get a scrape on your skin, be sure to wash it off and put an adhesive bandage on it. This helps protect you from germs. You (and an adult helper) can change the adhesive bandage as often as needed, until the cut heals.

Germs are not for sharing. Adults are probably always telling you to share your things, right? And so it may come as a surprise to hear that "germs are not for sharing." To help prevent the spread of colds and flu, make sure you don't share certain items—your toothbrush, juice boxes, lollipops, used tissues, or lip balm. Even if a friend asks you nicely to take a few licks from your candy or a sip from your drink, you can say no. You can remind your friend that germs are not for sharing.

Sneezing spreads germs. You can't help it if you have to sneeze. But guess what happens when you do? You spray tons of germs into the air. They travel incredibly fast, too—about 100 miles per hour. That's way faster than a car on the highway. Scientists say the germs can land as far away as the other side of the room! This is why it's so important to sneeze into a tissue and not on someone else. A tissue catches many of the germs so you don't share them with others. Wash your hands after sneezing, even if you sneezed into a tissue. And if you didn't have enough time to get a tissue and sneezed into your hands, wash them right away.

Coughing spreads germs. Just like when you sneeze, germs leave your body when you cough and they hit the air—or another person. So if you feel a cough coming, remember to cover it up. Grab a tissue and cough into it (wash your hands afterward). If you can't get a tissue fast enough, turn your face away from other people so they won't catch your germs. Cough into the crook of your elbow, so your sleeve can block the germs. And if you can't do that quick enough, turn your head toward your shoulder and cough into your shirt. Experts suggest always washing your hands after you cough or sneeze.

Hands spread germs. Your hands are busy all day long, writing, drawing, cutting, or throwing and catching a ball. But they're also catching germs and spreading them to others. You touch other people with your hands at home, at school, and lots of other places too. Every time you give someone a high five, you're sharing germs. Does that mean you should never touch anyone again? Of course not! But it's helpful to know that germs can be spread through touch.

Germs live on surfaces. Germs go from our hands to all the objects we touch, like pencils, doorknobs, and food. But did you know that germs can live on surfaces for quite a while—up to a few hours? Remember, most germs aren't harmful and you can touch them without getting ill. But if someone who *is* sick touches the things you touch, you may pick up some germs that you didn't want.

Washing your hands is a must. Experts say that keeping your hands clean is the most important thing you can do to keep from getting sick and spreading your germs to other people. On pages 24–25, you learned about 10 good times to wash your hands. Did you know that lots of people—adults included—don't wash their hands after using the bathroom? Or before they eat? You can do *your* part by washing your hands often during the day. Wash for about 30 seconds with warm water and soap. Be sure to rub your hands together. Wash between your fingers, too. Then rinse well and pat dry. Remind your brothers and sisters or your friends to do the same.

Keep an eye on your fingernails. Look at your fingernails … do they have dirt and sand under them? They probably do if you've been playing outside. Whenever you wash your hands, don't forget to clean under your nails. You can ask a grown-up to give you a nailbrush to help you get at the hard-to-reach parts.

Don't forget about me!

Watch where you put your fingers. Your fingertips have touched all sorts of stuff, and some of it may be pretty yucky. Avoid putting your fingers in your eyes, nose, or mouth unless you've washed them first. If you have to rub your eye and you know your fingers aren't clean, grab a tissue. And if that's not possible, rub your eye with your knuckle instead of your fingertip.

Watch what you put in your mouth. That piece of candy you find on the playground is crawling with germs. Yuck! Don't pick it up and eat it. Same goes for old bubblegum you find under a desk. Tell a grown-up what you found and ask him or her what to do about it. And if you ever accidentally drop your snack on the floor, it will be covered in germs by the time you pick it up (even if it touched the floor for just a second). Best bet: Go and get a new one.

Keep tissues handy and use them. You never know when you might need a tissue, so it's helpful to have some with you. You can keep them in your backpack, cubby, or pocket. Use them when you sneeze, cough, cry, wipe your eyes, or blow your nose.

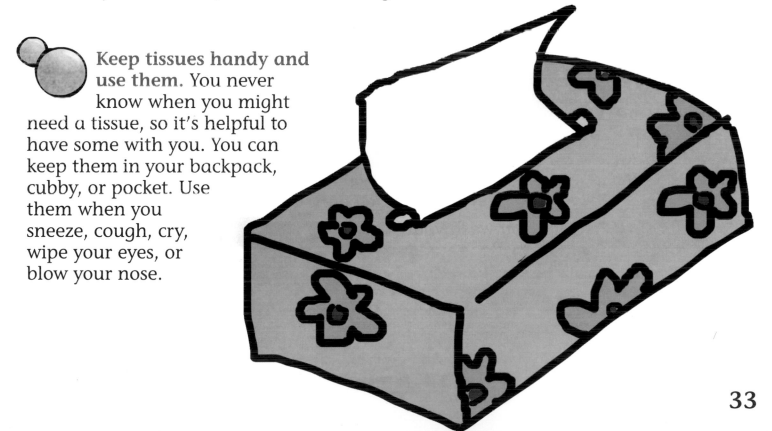

Keep the instant hand cleaner handy. You can't always find a sink when you need one. But you can keep hand-cleaning liquid or wipes with you for those times when you need to wash up. Ask your mom, dad, or another adult to buy some.

Be careful who you kiss. Maybe you love kissing your family members and friends (or maybe not!). Maybe you like to kiss your dog or other pets you know. Kisses can be nice to give and get—but there are times when you may want to think twice. For example, don't kiss people if you're sick or they are. Talk to a family grown-up about whether you're allowed to kiss your pets or other people's (animals have germs too).

Find other ways to stay clean and healthy. Grown-ups probably keep reminding you to wash your hands, brush your teeth, and eat healthy foods. And for good reason! When you stay clean and help take good care of yourself, you're healthier. And that means your body has a better chance of fighting off germs that could make you sick. That old saying "An apple a day keeps the doctor away" has some truth to it. You can do a lot to keep yourself healthy and strong!

For more on germs, check out this link:
www.scrubclub.org

About the Author and Illustrator

Elizabeth Verdick is the author of more than 30 highly acclaimed books for children and teenagers, including other books in the Best Behavior series for young children, the Toddler Tools board book series, and the Laugh & Learn series for preteens. Elizabeth lives with her husband, daughter, son, and five pets near St. Paul, Minnesota.

Marieka Heinlen launched her career as an award-winning children's book illustrator with the original edition of *Hands Are Not for Hitting* and has since illustrated many titles for young children, including other books in the Best Behavior series and the Toddler Tools board book series. As a freelance illustrator and designer, Marieka focuses her work on materials for children, teens, parents, and teachers. She lives in St. Paul, Minnesota, with her husband, son, and daughter.

Best Behavior™ English-Spanish Editions

Paperback (Ages 4–7)

Board Book

Hands Are Not for Hitting
Las manos no son para pegar

by Martine Agassi, Ph.D., illustrated by Marieka Heinlen

Hands are for helping, learning, playing, and much more. Children learn that hitting is never okay, hands can do many good things, and everyone is capable of positive, loving actions.

Paperback (Ages 4–7)

Board Book

Words Are Not for Hurting
Las palabras no son para lastimar

by Elizabeth Verdick, illustrated by Marieka Heinlen

With gentle encouragement, these books guide children to think before speaking, to choose words that are helpful instead of hurtful, and to say "I'm sorry" when hurtful words come out before kids can stop them.

Great Books from Free Spirit's Best Behavior™ Series

Simple words and delightful full-color illustrations guide children to choose peaceful, positive behaviors. Select titles are available in two versions: a durable board book for ages baby–preschool, and a longer, more in-depth paperback for ages 4–7. Kids, parents, and teachers will love these award-winning books. All include helpful tips for parents and caregivers.

Board Books: 24 pp., color illust., 7" x 7", ages baby–preschool

Diapers Are Not Forever
Learning to use the potty takes patience and practice, and this book helps pave the way. Young children learn how to use the potty and why it's time to do so.

Tails Are Not for Pulling
This book teaches the basics of kindness to animals: careful handling, awareness, safety, and respect.

Pacifiers Are Not Forever
This book smoothes the way and makes giving up the pacifier a positive experience for all.

Teeth Are Not for Biting
Sooner or later, almost all young children will bite someone—a friend, parent, or sibling. This upbeat book helps prevent biting and teaches positive alternatives.

Germs Are Not for Sharing
This book teaches the basics of not spreading germs: Cover up a sneeze or cough. Hug or blow kisses when you're sick. And most of all, wash your hands!

Words Are Not for Hurting
We can't expect children to watch every word, but we can help them understand that their words affect other people.

Hands Are Not for Hitting
Perfect for little hands—because it's never too early to learn that violence is never okay, hands can do many good things, and every child is capable of positive, loving actions.

Feet Are Not for Kicking
Helps little ones learn to use their feet for fun, not in anger or frustration. Includes tips on how to help toddlers be sweet with their feet.

Paperbacks: 40 pp., color illust., 9" x 9", ages 4–7

Hands Are Not for Hitting
Teaches children that violence is never okay, they can learn to manage their anger, and they are capable of positive, loving actions.

Tails Are Not for Pulling
Shows children how to love pets gently—because pets are for loving, after all! Kids learn that teasing isn't nice and they can choose to be kind to animals.

Words Are Not for Hurting
Encourages children to think before they speak, then choose what to say and how to say it.

Germs Are Not for Sharing
Helps kids understand what germs are, what they can do, and why it's so important to cover them up, keep them from spreading, and wash them down the drain.

For pricing information, to place an order, or to request a free catalog, contact:

Free Spirit Publishing Inc. • 217 Fifth Avenue North • Suite 200 • Minneapolis, MN 55401-1299
toll-free 800.735.7323 • local 612.338.2068 • fax 612.337.5050
help4kids@freespirit.com • www.freespirit.com